by Iain Gray

LangSyne

PUBLISHING

WRITING *to* REMEMBER

Lang**Syne**

PUBLISHING

WRITING *to* REMEMBER

E-mail: info@lang-syne.co.uk

Distributed in the Republic of Ireland by Portfolio Group,
Kilbarrack Ind. Est. Kilbarrack, Dublin 5.
T:00353(01) 839 4918 F:00353(01) 839 5826
sales@portfoliogroup.ie
www.portfoliogroup.ie

Design by Dorothy Meikle   Printed by Ricoh Print Scotland

ISBN 978-1-85217-316-6

Daly

MOTTO:
Faithful to my God and King
(and) Swift and strong.

CREST:
A greyhound in front of an oak tree.

NAME variations include:
Ó Dálaigh (*Gaelic*)
O'Dalaigh
O'Daly
Daley
Daily
Dailey
Dayley
Dawley

Chapter one:
Origins of Irish surnames

**According to an old saying, there are two types of Irish –
those who actually are Irish and those who wish they were.**

This sentiment is only one example of the allure that the
high romance and drama of the proud nation's history holds
for thousands of people scattered across the world today.

It's a sad fact, however, that the vast majority of Irish
surnames are found far beyond Irish shores, rather than on
the Emerald Isle itself.

The population stood at around eight million souls in
1841, but today it stands at fewer than six million.

This is mainly a tragic consequence of the potato
famine, also known as the Great Hunger, which devastated
Ireland between 1845 and 1849.

The Irish peasantry had become almost wholly reliant
for basic sustenance on the potato, first introduced from the
Americas in the seventeenth century.

When the crop was hit by a blight, at least 800,000
people starved to death while an estimated two million
others were forced to seek a new life far from their native
shores – particularly in America, Canada, and Australia.

The effects of the potato blight continued until about
1851, by which time a firm pattern of emigration had
become established.

Ireland's loss, however, was to the gain of the countries in which the immigrants settled, contributing enormously, as their descendants do today, to the well being of the nations in which their forefathers settled.

But those who were forced through dire circumstance to establish a new life in foreign parts never forgot their roots, or the proud heritage and traditions of the land that gave them birth.

Nor do their descendants.

It is a heritage that is inextricably bound up in the colourful variety of Irish names themselves – and the origin and history of these names forms an integral part of the vibrant drama that is the nation's history, one of both glorious fortune and tragic misfortune.

This history is well documented, and one of the most important and fascinating of the earliest sources are *The Annals of the Four Masters*, compiled between 1632 and 1636 by four friars at the Franciscan Monastery in County Donegal.

Compiled from earlier sources, and purporting to go back to the Biblical Deluge, much of the material takes in the mythological origins and history of Ireland and the Irish.

This includes tales of successive waves of invaders and settlers such as the Fomorians, the Partholonians, the Nemedians, the Fir Bolgs, the Tuatha De Danann, and the Laigain.

Of particular interest are the *Milesian Genealogies*,

because the majority of Irish clans today claim a descent from either Heremon, Ir, or Heber – three of the sons of Milesius, a king of what is now modern day Spain.

These sons invaded Ireland in the second millennium B.C, apparently in fulfilment of a mysterious prophecy received by their father.

This Milesian lineage is said to have ruled Ireland for nearly 3,000 years, until the island came under the sway of England's King Henry II in 1171 following what is known as the Cambro-Norman invasion.

This is an important date not only in Irish history in general, but for the effect the invasion subsequently had for Irish surnames.

'Cambro' comes from the Welsh, and 'Cambro-Norman' describes those Welsh knights of Norman origin who invaded Ireland.

But they were invaders who stayed, inter-marrying with the native Irish population and founding their own proud dynasties that bore Cambro-Norman names such as Archer, Barbour, Brannagh, Fitzgerald, Fitzgibbon, Fleming, Joyce, Plunkett, and Walsh – to name only a few.

These 'Cambro-Norman' surnames that still flourish throughout the world today form one of the three main categories in which Irish names can be placed – those of Gaelic-Irish, Cambro-Norman, and Anglo-Irish.

Previous to the Cambro-Norman invasion of the twelfth century, and throughout the earlier invasions and settlement of those wild bands of sea rovers known as the Vikings in the eighth and ninth centuries, the population of the island was relatively small, and it was normal for a person to be identified through the use of only a forename.

But as population gradually increased and there were many more people with the same forename, surnames were adopted to distinguish one person, or one community, from another.

Individuals identified themselves with their own particular tribe, or 'tuath', and this tribe – that also became known as a clann, or clan – took its name from some distinguished ancestor who had founded the clan.

The Gaelic-Irish form of the name Kelly, for example, is Ó Ceallaigh, or O'Kelly, indicating descent from an original 'Ceallaigh', with the 'O' denoting 'grandson of.' The name was later anglicised to Kelly.

The prefix 'Mac' or 'Mc', meanwhile, as with the clans of the Scottish Highlands, denotes 'son of.'

Although the Irish clans had much in common with their Scottish counterparts, one important difference lies in what are known as 'septs', or branches, of the clan.

Septs of Scottish clans were groups who often bore an entirely different name from the clan name but were under the clan's protection.

In Ireland, septs were groups that shared the same name and who could be found scattered throughout the four provinces of Ulster, Leinster, Munster, and Connacht.

The 'golden age' of the Gaelic-Irish clans, infused as their veins were with the blood of Celts, pre-dates the Viking invasions of the eighth and ninth centuries and the Norman invasion of the twelfth century, and the sacred heart of the country was the Hill of Tara, near the River Boyne, in County Meath.

Known in Gaelic as 'Teamhar na Rí', or Hill of Kings, it was the royal seat of the 'Ard Rí Éireann', or High King of Ireland, to whom the petty kings, or chieftains, from the island's provinces were ultimately subordinate.

It was on the Hill of Tara, beside a stone pillar known as the Irish 'Lia Fáil', or Stone of Destiny, that the High Kings were inaugurated and, according to legend, this stone would emit a piercing screech that could be heard all over Ireland when touched by the hand of the rightful king.

The Hill of Tara is today one of the island's main tourist attractions.

Opposition to English rule over Ireland, established in the wake of the Cambro-Norman invasion, broke out frequently and the harsh solution adopted by the powerful forces of the Crown was to forcibly evict the native Irish from their lands.

These lands were then granted to Protestant colonists, or 'planters', from Britain.

Many of these colonists, ironically, came from Scotland and were the descendants of the original 'Scotti', or 'Scots', who gave their name to Scotland after migrating there in the fifth century A.D., from the north of Ireland.

Colonisation entailed harsh penal laws being imposed on the majority of the native Irish population, stripping them practically of all of their rights.

The Crown's main bastion in Ireland was Dublin and its environs, known as the Pale, and it was the dispossessed peasantry who lived outside this Pale, desperately striving to eke out a meagre living.

It was this that gave rise to the modern-day expression of someone or something being 'beyond the pale'.

Attempts were made to stamp out all aspects of the ancient Gaelic-Irish culture, to the extent that even to bear a Gaelic-Irish name was to invite discrimination.

This is why many Gaelic-Irish names were anglicised with, for example, and noted above, Ó Ceallaigh, or O'Kelly, being anglicised to Kelly.

Succeeding centuries have seen strong revivals of Gaelic-Irish consciousness, however, and this has led to many families reverting back to the original form of their name, while the language itself is frequently found on the fluent tongues of an estimated 90,000 to 145,000 of the island's population.

Ireland's turbulent history of religious and political strife is one that lasted well into the twentieth century, a landmark century that saw the partition of the island into the twenty-six counties of the independent Republic of

Ireland, or Eire, and the six counties of Northern Ireland, or Ulster.

Dublin, originally founded by Vikings, is now a vibrant and truly cosmopolitan city while the proud city of Belfast is one of the jewels in the crown of Ulster.

It was Saint Patrick who first brought the light of Christianity to Ireland in the fifth century A.D.

Interpretations of this Christian message have varied over the centuries, often leading to bitter sectarian conflict – but the many intricately sculpted Celtic Crosses found all over the island are symbolic of a unity that crosses the sectarian divide.

It is an image that fuses the 'old gods' of the Celts with Christianity.

All the signs from the early years of this new millennium indicate that sectarian strife may soon become a thing of the past – with the Irish and their many kinsfolk across the world, be they Protestant or Catholic, finding common purpose in the rich tapestry of their shared heritage.

Chapter two:
Of royal race

One clue to the possible origin of the Daly name can be found in the Gaelic-Irish name for the parliament of the Republic of Ireland.

This is Dáil Éireann, with 'dáil' signifying a place where meetings or assemblies are held, while the Gaelic-Irish form of Daly is Ó Dálaigh, again derived from the root word 'dáil.'

It is certainly more than mere coincidence that the Ó Dálaighs were renowned for centuries as bards, or poets, who would recite their works at assemblies of their kinsfolk.

Although to be found in other parts of the island that included County Galway, their main territory was the area of present day Westmeath, near the sacred Hill of Tara where the ancient Ard Rí, or High Kings, were solemnly inaugurated.

This is rather fitting, because royal blood courses through the veins of the Dalys themselves, descended as they are from one of the island's earliest monarchs.

This was Heremon who, along with his brothers Heber, Ir and Amergin the Druid and four other brothers, was a son of Milesius, a king of what is now modern day Spain, and who had planned to invade the Emerald Isle in fulfilment of a mysterious Druidic prophecy.

Milesius died before he could embark on the invasion

but his sons, including Heremon, Heber, Ir and Amergin, successfully undertook the daunting task in his stead in about 1699B.C.

Legend holds that their invasion fleet was scattered in a storm and Ir killed when his ship was driven onto the island of Scellig-Mhicheal, off the coast of modern day Co. Kerry.

Only Heremon, Heber, and Amergin survived, although Ir left issue.

Heremon and Heber became the first of the Milesian monarchs of Ireland, but Heremon later killed Heber in a quarrel caused by their wives, while Amergin was slain by Heremon in an argument over territory.

Adding even more lustre to the royal pedigree of the Dalys is that they were of the tribal grouping known as the southern Uí Neill, indicating a descent from one of Ireland's greatest warrior kings.

This was Niall Noíghiallach, better known to posterity as Niall of the Nine Hostages.

The dramatic life and times of this ancestor of the Dalys are steeped in stirring Celtic myth and legend.

The youngest son of Eochaidh Mugmedon, king of the province of Connacht, his mother died in childbirth and he was brought up by his evil stepmother Mongfhinn who was determined that he should die.

She accordingly abandoned him naked on the Hill of Tara, but he was found by a wandering bard who took him back to his father.

One legend is that Mongfhinn sent Niall and his four brothers – Brian, Fiachra, Ailill, and Fergus – to a renowned prophet who was also a blacksmith to determine which of them would succeed their father as Ard Rí.

The blacksmith, known as Sitchin, set the lads a task by deliberately setting fire to his forge.

Niall's brothers ran in and came out carrying the spearheads, fuel, hammers, and barrels of beer that they had rescued, but Niall staggered out clutching the heavy anvil so vital to the blacksmith's trade.

By this deed, Sitchin prophesied that Niall would be the one who would take on the glorious mantle of kingship.

Another prophetic incident occurred one day while Niall and his brothers were engaged in the hunt.

Thirsty from their efforts, they encountered an ugly old woman who offered them water – but only in return for a kiss.

Three of the lads, no doubt repelled by her green teeth and scaly skin, refused; Fiachra pecked her lightly on the cheek and, by this act, she prophesied that he would one day reign at Tara – but only briefly.

The bold Niall, however, kissed her fully on the lips; the hag then demanded that he should now have full sexual intercourse with her and, undaunted, he did so.

Through this action she was suddenly transformed into a stunningly beautiful young woman known as Flaithius, or Royalty, who predicted that he would become the greatest High King of Ireland.

His stepmother Mongfhinn later tried to poison him, but accidentally took the deadly potion herself and died.

This legend relates to what was known as the Festival of Mongfhinn, or Feis na Samhan (the Feast of Samhain), because it was on the evening of October 31, on Samhain's Eve, that the poisoning incident is said to have taken place.

It was believed for centuries in Ireland that, on Samhain Eve, Mongfhinn's warped and wicked spirit would roam the land in hungry search of children's souls.

The Festival, or Feast, of Samhain, is better known today as Halloween.

Niall became Ard Rí in 379 A.D. and embarked on the series of military campaigns and other daring adventures that would subsequently earn him the title of Niall of the Nine Hostages.

The nine countries and territories into which he raided and took hostages for ransom were the Irish provinces of Munster, Leinster, Connacht, and Ulster, Britain, and the territories of the Saxons, Morini, Picts, and Dalriads.

But while it is commonly accepted that it was through his raids on nine different territories and countries that Niall acquired the 'Niall of the Nine Hostages' appellation, it is also a curious fact that the Celts placed a particular significance on the number nine.

They were aware, for example, that if you stand on any seashore and count the waves as they break on the shore, you would notice after a time that it is always the ninth wave in the sequence that is the highest.

Niall's most famous hostage, meanwhile, was a young lad known as Succat, son of Calpernius, a Romano-Briton who lived in the area of present day Milford Haven, on the Welsh coast.

Later known as Patricius, or Patrick, he became renowned as Ireland's patron saint, St. Patrick, responsible for bringing the light of Christianity to the island in the early years of the fifth century A.D.

Raiding in Gaul, in the area of Boulogne-sur-mer in present day France, Niall was ambushed and killed by one of his treacherous subjects in 405 A.D.

But his legacy survived through the royal dynasties and clans, such as the Dalys, that were founded by his brothers and sons.

Away from the field of battle it was as poets and scholars that the Dalys gained great distinction, expertly knowledge-able as they were of ancient Celtic tradition.

Chapter three:

Bards and scholars

One distinguished ancestor of the Dalys was the sixth century Dálach, who served as hereditary bard, or poet, to the kings of the province of Munster.

These bards, or *fili*, played a hugely important role in Celtic society, tasked as they were with the recording and compilation of a clan's genealogy and committing the glorious deeds of chieftains and their warriors to verse.

Rooted in the ancient Druidic tradition, the *fili* were capable of prodigious feats of memory, able to remember hundreds of poems and tales that they would recite around a blazing fire to their awed listeners on dark winter nights.

It was bards such as Dálach who were the authors of the traditional Irish tales that are now grouped in what are known as *The Mythological Cycle*, *The Fenian Cycle* and *The Ulster Cycle*.

One particularly famous compilation of early Irish verse is the *Leabhar Gabhála*, or *Book of Invasions*, and the following few lines from this impressive work give a flavour of the colourful and imaginative verse of which the bards were undisputed masters:

> *I am the wind that blows over the sea,*
> *I am the wave of the ocean,*
> *I am the murmur of the billows,*

> *I am the ox of the seven combats,*
> *I am the vulture on the rock,*
> *I am a ray of the sun…*

Another noted Daly bard was Donnchadh Mór Ó Dálaigh, who died in 1244, and who is described in *The Annals of the Four Masters* as 'a poet who never was, and never will be, surpassed', and in more recent times as 'the Irish Ovid.'

He was a brother of Muiredagh Ó Dálaigh, the early thirteenth century bard who was forced to seek refuge with the MacDonalds of Clanranald of the island of Islay, off the west coast of Scotland.

The rather hot-tempered poet had been forced to flee his native land after killing a steward of the powerful clan O'Donnell who had had the temerity to demand that he pay his taxes.

Appointed chief poet to the MacDonalds of Clanranald, he later became the founder of the Scottish Clan MacMhuirich, or MacVurrach, also known as Currie.

Another particularly noted Daly bard and scholar was Cuconnacht na Scoile O'Dalaigh, or 'Cuconnacht of the School' who, by the time of his death in 1139, had founded a school for bards and minstrels.

So renowned were the Dalys as bards that many became hereditary bards to clans outwith their own territory, as was the case with Dálach, who served as bard to the MacCarthys of Munster.

In East Bréifne, now modern day Co. Cavan, they were bards to the proud Clan O'Reilly, while in the province of Connacht they were hereditary bards to the Royal House of O'Connor.

The way of life of Gaelic-Irish clans such as the Dalys was rocked to its ancient foundations in the late twelfth century in the wake of the Norman invasion of the island and the subsequent consolidation of the power of the English Crown.

English dominion over Ireland was ratified through the Treaty of Windsor of 1175, under the terms of which native Irish chieftains were allowed to rule territory unoccupied by the Normans only in the role of a vassal of the king.

What was ultimately created over time were actually three separate Irelands.

These were the territories of the privileged and powerful Norman barons and their retainers, the Ireland of the disaffected Gaelic-Irish who held lands unoccupied by the Normans, and the Pale – comprised of Dublin itself and a substantial area of its environs ruled over by an English elite.

Ireland groaned under a weight of oppression that was directed in the main against the native Irish clans such as the Dalys.

An indication of the harsh treatment meted out to them can be found in a desperate plea sent to Pope John XII by Roderick O'Carroll of Ely, Donald O'Neill of Ulster, and a number of other Irish chieftains in 1318.

They stated: 'As it very constantly happens, whenever an Englishman, by perfidy or craft, kills an Irishman, however noble, or however innocent, be he clergy or layman, there is no penalty or correction enforced against the person who may be guilty of such wicked murder.

'But rather the more eminent the person killed and the higher rank which he holds among his own people, so much more is the murderer honoured and rewarded by the English, and not merely by the people at large, but also by the religious and bishops of the English race.'

This appeal to the Pope had no effect whatsoever on English policy and many clans frequently resorted to rebellion.

Others, walking a tightrope between preserving their ancient rights and traditions and the haughty demands of the English Crown, sought some form of accommodation with the ruling power.

This often took the form of changing their Gaelic-Irish name to one more 'acceptable' to English ears and by swearing reluctant allegiance to the Crown.

This explains the Daly motto of 'Faithful to my God and King' but, rather intriguingly and not commonly known to bearers of the name today, there is an even older motto.

This is 'Swift and strong' – a motto that was retained for centuries by the sept of the O'Dalys of Dunsandle, in Co. Galway.

One look at the Daly crest, featuring a fleet greyhound

in front of a flourishing oak tree, explains why 'Swift and strong' may well have been the original motto of the clan and this is why it is included as such in this brief history of the Dalys.

The crest is also one of the features incised on what is known as the Daly Stone, or the O'Daly Marriage Stone.

Regarded by experts as a truly unique example of early seventeenth century stone art and incorporating intricate religious symbolism, it is believed to have originally formed part of a mantelpiece installed during the reconstruction of Killimor Castle in 1624 by the O'Daly chieftain Teige O'Daly and his beloved wife Sisily.

The castle was demolished in the late seventeenth century following the abortive Irish Jacobite War of 1688 to 1691 and replaced by Killimor House, where the stone was inserted into a wall.

By about 1800 it was taken to Dunsandle House, in Co. Galway and in the early 1980s, following a period at Clogham Castle in Co. Offaly, it was placed outside the entrance to the graveyard of Killimordaly Parish Church – where it is admired by hundreds of tourists to the area every year.

The virtual destruction of the ancient Gaelic way of life of clans such as the Dalys followed in the wake of the Irish Jacobite War, when a series of measures known as the Penal Laws were put into effect.

Under their terms Catholics were barred from the legal

profession, the armed forces, and parliament, not allowed to bear arms or own a horse worth more than £5, barred from running their own schools and from sending their children abroad for their education.

All Roman Catholic clergy and bishops were officially 'banished' from the island in 1697, while it has been estimated that by 1703 less than 15% of the land throughout the entire island was owned by Irish Catholics.

Some sought a new life in foreign lands while others converted to the Protestant faith – but both Catholics and some Protestants found a tenuous measure of solidarity following controversial policies that threatened the traditional agrarian economy.

Born in the small townland of Rahruddy, west of Loughrea in Co. Galway, Anthony Daly was a prominent member of what was known and feared as the Whiteboy movement.

'Whiteboy', 'Rightboys', 'Peep O'Day Boys', 'Thrashers' and 'Rockites' were the names given to small Irish landholders such as Anthony Daly who engaged in militant protest against land enclosures, high rents and evictions.

Taking oaths of secrecy and dressed in white shirts, or smocks – hence the name ''Whiteboys '' – they chose the dead of night to tear down the stone walls that had been erected to enclose land and to terrorise the major landowners.

Arrested and found guilty of attempted murder in 1820, Daly was duly hanged, while his life and times later became the subject of a poem by James Stephens and a celebrated choral work by the composer Samuel Barber.

A champion of rather more peaceful means to achieve land reform was James Daly, the Irish nationalist who was born in Co. Mayo in 1838 and who died in 1910.

A staunch supporter of the rights of tenant farmers, he was instrumental in the formation in 1879 of the influential Irish National Land League.

Chapter four:
On the world stage

From acting and sport to literature, science and the military, generations of bearers of the proud Daly name have gained distinction in a wide range of endeavours.

Born in 1918 in Wisconsin Rapids, Wisconsin, **James Daly** was the award-winning American theatre, television, and film actor who is best remembered for his role in the television series *Medical Center*, while from 1953 to 1955 he also appeared in the equally popular series *Foreign Intrigue*.

A regular guest star on television series that included *Mission: Impossible*, *The Twilight Zone*, *Gunsmoke*, and *The Virginian*, the actor, who died in 1978, was married to the actress Hope Newell from 1942 to 1965.

One of their children is the actress **Tyne Daly**, born Ellen Tyne Daly in 1946 in Madison, Wisconsin.

An Emmy and a Tony award-winning actress, she is best known for her role in the 1980s as Mary Beth Lacey in the police drama *Cagney and Lacey*, while earlier she starred beside Clint Eastwood in the 1976 film *The Enforcer*.

She is the recipient of four Emmys for Leading Actress in a Drama Series for *Cagney and Lacey*, one for Best Supporting Actress in a Drama Series for the 1996 *Christy*, and one for Best Supporting Actress in a Drama Series for the 2003 *Judging Amy*.

A Tony Award for Best Actress in a Musical came in 1990 for her portrayal of Madame Rose in *Gypsy*.

She is the sister of the Emmy-nominated stage, screen and voice actor, director and producer **Timothy Daly**, born in 1956 in New York City, and whose film roles include the 1982 *Diner*, the 1996 *The Associate* and the 2008 *The Skeptic*.

Born in 1963, **Candice Daly** was the American film and television actress who starred in a number of B-movies during the late 1980s and early 1990s, including the 1988 cult film *After Death* and the 1991 *Liquid Dreams*.

The actress, who later starred in the American television soap *The Young and the Restless*, died in 2004.

Over the ocean to Britain, **Tess Daly**, born in 1971 in Stockport, Cheshire, is the television presenter who, along with Bruce Forsyth, has hosted the popular *Strictly Come Dancing* series and who is married to fellow television presenter Vernon Kay.

Once one of the most recognised voices on American radio and television, **John Daly** was the journalist and author born in 1914 in Johannesburg, South Africa.

He first came to the attention of American radio audiences in the 1930s and early 1940s as the CBS network's announcer for many of President Franklin Roosevelt's speeches from the White House, while he was also the first national radio correspondent to announce the news of Japan's attack on Pearl Harbor on December 7, 1941.

Daly, who was also the first on radio to announce the

president's death on April 12, 1945, later became the host of pioneering television panel shows such as *What's My Line?*

He died in 1991.

A renowned television host of more recent times is **Carson Daly**, born in 1973 in Santa Monica, California. Formerly a host of MTV's *Total Request Live* show, at the time of writing he hosts NBC's *Last Call with Carson Daly*.

Born in 1838 in Plymouth, North Carolina, **John Augustan Daly** was the innovative American theatrical manager and playwright who in 1879 built and opened Daly's Theatre in New York, followed fourteen years later by Daly's Theatre in London.

Daly, who died in 1899, was the author of a number of plays that included *Under the Gaslight*.

Also in the world of literature **Maureen Daly**, born in Co. Tyrone in 1921 but who was raised in Fond du Lac, Wisconsin, was the Irish-American author best known for her 1942 novel *Seventeenth Summer* – recognised as the first of a genre addressed specifically to a teenage audience.

Awarded the American Freedom Foundation Medal in 1952, she died fourteen years later.

Dalys have also excelled in the highly competitive world of sport.

Born in 1891 in St. John, New Brunswick, **Thomas Daly** was the Canadian Major League Baseball player who was a famed catcher for the Chicago White Sox from 1913 to 1915 and the Chicago Cubs from 1918 to 1921.

Daly, who later managed the Toronto Maple Leafs, died in 1946.

In baseball **Chuck Daly**, born in 1930 in St. Mary's, Pennsylvania, is the former top American head coach who was inducted into the Baseball Hall of Fame in 1994.

He is best known for coaching the Detroit Pistons for nine years, during which period, in 1989 and 1990, they won consecutive NBA championships, and for coaching the U.S team that won gold at the 1992 Olympics.

In hurling **Anthony Daly**, born in 1970 in Clarecastle, Co. Clare, is the manager and former player who is recognised as one of the county's greatest ever players, while also in the Irish Republic **Derek Daley**, born in 1953 in Dublin, is the former racing driver who won the 1977 British Formula Three Championship.

On the golf course **Fred Daly**, born in 1911 in Portrush, Co. Antrim and who died in 1990, was the Northern Irish professional golfer who won the 1947 Open Championship and played in a number of Ryder Cups between 1947 and 1953.

Also on the golf course John Daly, born in 1966 in Carmichael, California, and better known by his nickname of **Long Tom Daly**, is the American professional golfer who won the 1991 PGA Championship.

In European football **Jon Daly** is the Irish striker born in 1983 in Dublin and who, at the time of writing, plays for Dundee United in the Scottish Premier League.

In American football **Charles Daly**, better known as Dan Daly, was the player and coach who was born in Boston in 1880 and who died in 1959.

Attending both Harvard University and West Point Military Academy, he played football for both institutions and later became a coach at West Point – coaching such outstanding future American Army officers as Dwight D. Eisenhower and George S. Patton.

An athletic field at West Point, where he also taught as an assistant professor of military science and tactics, is named in his honour.

In the ecclesiastical sphere, **Cahal Daly**, born in 1917 in Loughguile, Co. Armagh, is the Roman Catholic prelate who, after being ordained to the priesthood in 1941, served as Archbishop of Armagh and Cardinal Primate of All Ireland from 1990 to 1996.

In the world of scientific research, **Marie Maynard Daly**, born in 1921 in Queens, New York City, was awarded a doctorate from Columbia University in 1947 – making her the first African-American woman to earn a Ph.D. in chemistry.

A pioneer in the study of the effects of cigarette smoking on the lungs, she died in 2003.

On the field of battle, **Sergeant Major Daniel Daly**, born in 1873 in Glen Cove, New York, was the United States Marine who was a recipient on two separate occasions of the Medal of Honor.

The first time was for single-handedly defending a position during the Boxer Rebellion in 1910 in what was then Peking, China, while the second was in 1905 for fighting off a group of 400 Haitian bandits who had ambushed him and his 35 comrades.

He is also famously remembered for his actions during the First World War when, during the battle of Belleau Wood in France, he rallied his besieged men and led them in a successful counter-attack with the cry 'Come on, you sons of bitches, do you want to live for ever?'

Sergeant Major Daly, who was awarded the Navy Cross for this action, died in 1937.

One particularly infamous bearer of the Daly name was the American Wild West outlaw **John Daly**.

Born in 1839, he arrived in Nevada territory in the early 1860s and, with his gunslinging band of fellow outlaws feared as the Daly Gang, terrorised the peaceful citizens of the townships of Aurora and Carson City for two years.

But it was not until the murder in February 1864, of townsman William R. Johnston, who had killed Daly Gang member Jim Sears, that Nevada citizens plucked up the courage to band together and form the Citizens' Protective Association.

This move sounded the death knell of the Daly Gang – with John Daly and three other gang members captured and summarily hanged within only a week of the formation of the association.

Key dates in Ireland's history from the first settlers to the formation of the Irish Republic:

circa 7000 B.C.	Arrival and settlement of Stone Age people.
circa 3000 B.C.	Arrival of settlers of New Stone Age period.
circa 600 B.C.	First arrival of the Celts.
200 A.D.	Establishment of Hill of Tara, Co. Meath, as seat of the High Kings.
circa 432 A.D.	Christian mission of St. Patrick.
800-920 A.D.	Invasion and subsequent settlement of Vikings.
1002 A.D.	Brian Boru recognised as High King.
1014	Brian Boru killed at battle of Clontarf.
1169-1170	Cambro-Norman invasion of the island.
1171	Henry II claims Ireland for the English Crown.
1366	Statutes of Kilkenny ban marriage between native Irish and English.
1529-1536	England's Henry VIII embarks on religious Reformation.
1536	Earl of Kildare rebels against the Crown.
1541	Henry VIII declared King of Ireland.
1558	Accession to English throne of Elizabeth I.
1565	Battle of Affane.
1569-1573	First Desmond Rebellion.
1579-1583	Second Desmond Rebellion.
1594-1603	Nine Years War.
1606	Plantation' of Scottish and English settlers.

1607	Flight of the Earls.
1632-1636	Annals of the Four Masters compiled.
1641	Rebellion over policy of plantation and other grievances.
1649	Beginning of Cromwellian conquest.
1688	Flight into exile in France of Catholic Stuart monarch James II as Protestant Prince William of Orange invited to take throne of England along with his wife, Mary.
1689	William and Mary enthroned as joint monarchs; siege of Derry.
1690	Jacobite forces of James defeated by William at battle of the Boyne (July) and Dublin taken.
1691	Athlone taken by William; Jacobite defeats follow at Aughrim, Galway, and Limerick; conflict ends with Treaty of Limerick (October) and Irish officers allowed to leave for France.
1695	Penal laws introduced to restrict rights of Catholics; banishment of Catholic clergy.
1704	Laws introduced constricting rights of Catholics in landholding and public office.
1728	Franchise removed from Catholics.
1791	Foundation of United Irishmen republican movement.
1796	French invasion force lands in Bantry Bay.
1798	Defeat of Rising in Wexford and death of United Irishmen leaders Wolfe Tone and Lord Edward Fitzgerald.

1800	Act of Union between England and Ireland.
1803	Dublin Rising under Robert Emmet.
1829	Catholics allowed to sit in Parliament.
1845-1849	The Great Hunger: thousands starve to death as potato crop fails and thousands more emigrate.
1856	Phoenix Society founded.
1858	Irish Republican Brotherhood established.
1873	Foundation of Home Rule League.
1893	Foundation of Gaelic League.
1904	Foundation of Irish Reform Association.
1913	Dublin strikes and lockout.
1916	Easter Rising in Dublin and proclamation of an Irish Republic.
1917	Irish Parliament formed after Sinn Fein election victory.
1919-1921	War between Irish Republican Army and British Army.
1922	Irish Free State founded, while six northern counties remain part of United Kingdom as Northern Ireland, or Ulster; civil war up until 1923 between rival republican groups.
1949	Foundation of Irish Republic after all remaining constitutional links with Britain are severed.